HAUNTED AUGUSTA AND LOCAL LEGENDS

BY

SEAN JOINER

Llumina Press

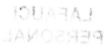

ISBN: 1-932047-97-2.

Printed in the United States of America.

This book is dedicated to my loving wife, Holly.

TABLE OF CONTENTS

ACKNOWLEDGEMENT

I would like to thank my wife Holly for her support while I wrote *Haunted Augusta and Local Legends*. You encouraged me more than you will ever know. When I first started writing the book, I never thought it would see the light of day. As time passed I watched the book grow page by page and soon it became a reality.

I would like to thank Dr. Gerald Smith for his guidance while I wrote this work. The forward you supplied for the book helps to bring so much to the stories that it holds. Thank you for your expertise.

Finally, I want to thank all of the people past and present who have made Augusta and the surrounding communities the wonderful places they are.

The Celtic Cross at St. Paul's Church commemorates the founding of Augusta.

INTRODUCTION

I n April of 2001 I traveled to Williamsburg, Virginia, with my wife, Holly, on vacation. History has always been appealing to me and this was a chance to view one of the most historical sites in this great country. During the weeklong trip I was able to hear the many folktales, legends, and hauntings that flow through the historic triangle. After arriving back in Augusta, I thought back to my childhood and the stories my grandparents told me about Augusta. Being a lifelong resident, I have had many conversations over the years with people in reference to local hauntings and legends. I soon realized that these accounts were not together in a volume for people to enjoy, so that was the start of this project.

Traveling long hours can be exhausting, so Holly and I stopped at her aunt's house in Chatham, Virginia to spend the night. One of the oldest houses in Virginia, it also stands as one of the most beautiful I have seen and is rich in its history. There are old stories that accompany any historic house and the ones attributed to this one I'd heard several times since meeting my wife. I must admit every time the stories were retold, my interest would grow. So again the desire to share stories of the Augusta area strengthened. At this juncture I decided to write the book you hold in your hands.

My grandmother passed away in December 2001 while I was at work. When the phone rang I received news of her passing and immediately headed to the hospital. I learned of a strange event that took place before her death and began to think there are questions to be answered. I spoke to a man that had been in the hospital room visiting another patient. His account of what transpired was soul shaking. He related that my grandmother had sat up in bed, looked at him, called out a name, and told him to call that person. Before he knew what happened she lay in a quiet and peaceful state. Surprised at the name she called out, the man knew immediately who she was talking about. Strangely enough the woman my grandmother referred to was someone that knew the family and the man in the room had met my grandmother years before.

Christmas was approaching and it was going to be a tough holiday season. Holly and I went back home. The late night hours slowly approached as I sat on the couch watching television and thinking of my grandmother. I had placed a poinsettia on a shelf next to other festive holiday decorations. Moments after thoughts of her filled my head, I saw the plant fall from the shelf. In my opinion the poinsettia could not have fallen on its own after being placed near the back and not the edge of the shelf. Sometimes it seems this may have been her way of saying that everything would be fine and just a little reminder she would be there watching over me.

This story is an example of an event that happened and will be told to my children and their children. One day it will be considered legend, at least in my family. Every person, town, and city have stories to tell, whether they are locked in the past behind doors of an old house or listed publicly on markers in plain view for all eyes to see. Whether these stories are current or hidden in the past, they make up the foundations of our local culture.

This book is for the enjoyment of the reader. Stories

passed down about Augusta and the areas surrounding this great city is a birthright for all those living here. Anyone reading this book should not confuse its purpose. Convincing people of the existence of the supernatural is not the intent, but fulfillment of history, and curiosity is its mission. I hope you enjoy these fascinating tales.

Sean Joiner

FORWARD

"Backward, turn backward
O Time in thy flight—
Make me a child again
Once for tonight."

Henry Wadsworth Longfellow penned these lines with the backward glance that yearns within human beings for a more stable existence. It is really the quest for performance in the ever-shifting scenes of life that time forces on us. Be it an hourglass, an old watch, or the ultramodern quartz gizmos with glowing numbers, we are constantly reminded that time is fleeting, history moving ever forward, the Devil—or whatever we as moderns choose to call him these days—take the hindmost. We, in the few moments we grasp for reflection, are breathless, too winded perhaps to reflect at all. The modern credo is to exist—for no true living can be done—at ninety miles an hour just to keep up. We are in effect caught between the past and what might be just around the corner. The present tense of our lives is a blur of velocity and mass.

No wonder, then, that so many people today are more and more interested in antiques—old houses, old furniture, old knick-knacks: all of these things bear for us the unmistakable aura of a more earnest time, now forever gone by, when there was a modicum of stability. Like a ship at sea beset by storms, we want an anchor to steady the pitching and rolling of our lives, and these old things help to do that. Do we dare speak the word for this? Nostalgia, that most human of attributes, often scorned as silly, is like a balm for the hurried spirit, as surely a medicine as anything a physician ever prescribed.

"Make me a child again..." the poet opines wistfully. What a lovely thought. The dreaming over the old Sears Roebuck "Wishbook" at Christmas, the ghost stories told over campfires, the goose-pimply shiver in an old deserted house—there was one house at least in all small towns which was whispered around as "haunted". The strange affection for old heroisms—those things, and hundreds more which could be named, are the stuff of nostalgia. Surely living in the past may be harmful, we are told, but relinquishing the past is something else again. We dare not give it up. For the past is ours and the past is us.

The stories in the following pages will bring a sense of nostalgia to the reader—ghosts, heroes, old houses, on and on. Read them with a sense of pleasure, for in doing so, for a few minutes at least, life will slow down, take on meaning in the process, and while it is patently preposterous that we might become children again, as the poet has it, we will at least recover something of the simplicity and stability of childhood when life still had for each of us that innocence and faith before reality set in, and our lovely dreams took on all the fierceness of nightmare.

Gerald J. Smith Ph.D.

Haunted Pillar

THE HAUNTED PILLAR

Standing in defiance on the corner of Broad and Fifth Street is a lone stone column. Seemingly ageless, the weathered structure is the remnant of the Lower Market that once stood near the area. Augusta's economic blood pulsed through the Lower Market. When one would stand at one end of Broad Street, the clock resting inside the tall tower overlooking the market could be seen with ease. Business was conducted through the selling of agriculture, livestock, and slaves. The first building housing the Lower Market burned and soon a second building was erected. Without sympathy, violent destruction befell the market again.

Local legend tells of a preacher who rode into Augusta in 1829. Light shown brightly through the heavens on this sunny day while people were busily enthralled with their daily activities. Yelling in an attempt to overcome noise made by the crowd, the preacher demanded Augusta build him a church so he could preach his message of redemption. Mocking him, the crowd went about their business. He became furious and issued a curse upon Augusta and its populace. Condemnation set forth by the preacher gave appointment to the destruction of the Lower Market. A great wind would bring down the formidable foe, with only one pillar remaining upright. Anyone touching or attempting to remove the pillar would die.

On February 8, 1878, a strange darkness pushed the sun from the heavens. A cyclone set down on the Lower Market, ripping it from the foundation. Amongst the wreckage stood one pillar.

In 1879, a town hall was built where the Lower Market had once stood. Local grocer, Theodore Eye, bought the pillar for fifty dollars, and moved it to the location where it now stands. Lightning strikes and automobile accidents have plagued the column since its removal from the rubble, each time to be promptly repaired.

Downtown residents reflect on stories of people being struck by lightning while standing next to the pillar, footsteps heard following the passersby, and a mysterious handprint appearing from nothingness resting on the cold stone.

Workers began to clear debris from the streets where the tornado had set down on the market. One man having heard the curse laughed, put a rope around the pillar, and then died from a heart attack while he attempted to topple it. Another story tells of Broad Street when it was being widened. Two workmen tied ropes around the pillar and were immediately struck by lightning, causing both men to die.

There is a tale that gives account to an incident that happened on June, 13, 1958 which provides an interesting outlook on the legend of the pillar. A truck hauling cotton sped around the corner where the pillar sits. Falling from the truck, a loose bale of cotton struck the pillar causing part of it to collapse. With bricks lying on the ground, temptation for a souvenir was too much for a passerby walking down the street. He quickly grabbed the stonework and walked off with his prize. Apparently within the hour he passed out for some unknown reason. Not taking any chances with the curse, he returned the brick to where he had found it.

Some say there is the residue of a curse uttered by a man being sold into slavery. Resting a bloody hand on the pillar holding him prisoner, the slave called for justice to avenge the mistreatment he suffered at uncaring hands.

Years later a gold seeker named J.H. Winfrey looked feverishly for gold that was supposed to be buried near the site of the old pillar. He was also known as a water witch and claimed that he was on the verge of finding great amounts of treasure if it had not been for the city workers repairing the holes in the pavement.

Most people thought Winfrey to be out of his mind with the claims of hearing voices, seeing spirits, and holding his odd treasure wand before him claiming to have found something worthwhile. Lunacy caused him to be arrested many times, at which point he claimed it was the fault of the police that he lost the gold he had just located moments before.

Perhaps handprints do appear on the pillar, but only to a select few. Footsteps heard in the distance by unsuspecting visitors might be the preacher still looking for a place to preach. Most people approach the pillar with curiosity, but keep their distance just in case the curse is true.

Indian Tomb at St. Paul's Church

GHOST RIDER ON
REYNOLDS STREET

Augusta was a wooded frontier when it was founded in 1735. Fur traders dotted the landscape with makeshift trading posts, living side by side with local Indians. The new settlement was given the name Augusta after Princess Augusta.

A fort was built near the banks of the Savannah River to protect the newcomers and their homes. As settlers increased, it was decided the need for a church was in order and in 1750 St. Paul's Church was built. Because tensions with the Indians could at any time start to strain, the church was built in the shadows of the fort to procure protection from its weapons. The quaint building was made of wood and plaster with Jonathan Copp being sent as the first rector.

Over the years the church has been destroyed four times and each time rebuilt. After the destruction of the first church by a fire that started from a battle with British forces, a new church was built also made of wood, with the first brick building being erected in 1820. This building stood until a great fire ravaged Augusta in 1916 and burned the soon to be century old building to the ground. In 1919, a new church was built in a Colonial Georgian style and has remained as a house of worship with a stable congregation throughout the years.

In the nave of the church some of Augusta's oldest artifacts are on display. There is a baptismal font sitting in a protected area that was saved from the fire of 1916 that dates back to the first church, along with several items encased in glass representing the history of the church.

Outside of the church is Augusta's oldest cemetery. Buried on the grounds are the people who struggled to make Augusta the thriving city it is today. Some of the most important contributors to the city and the United States are buried here. Among them rests the remains of William Few, a local patriot, who signed the United States Constitution.

On the south corner of the graveyard in front of the church stands a tall brick structure covered by ivy. It is said that an Indian chief is buried here sitting on his horse. The rider and his companion are entombed in brick for eternity.

In the early morning hours, especially when a full moon hovers in the sky, people tell stories of seeing a ghost horse being ridden by an Indian chief screaming his war cry while riding down Reynolds Street and then disappearing into nothingness. He holds his weapons high above his head showing no fear as if he is readying himself for some unseen battle.

Others tell the true story of the structure being that of a Masonic pyramid built many years ago. The eye once sitting on top overlooking the yard is gone. According to some local residents, the tale of the Indian chief being buried in the cemetery is only a story that was told to Sunday school children many years ago when Augusta was young.

Whether it is a story told to children on Sundays or a symbol of the Masonic order, many people will argue the point, telling stories of ancestors seeing the ghost ride down the street in front of the church. Others claim to have seen him themselves. So if it is late at night, the moon full, and Reynolds Street quiet, look for the ghostly figure of the Indian chief riding into the night looking for his eternal battle.

Old Medical College of Georgia

RE/URRECTION MAN

n 1829, the Medical Academy of Georgia was opened in Augusta with three doctors and a small number of students. The academy was allowed to bestow medical degrees on students and changed its name to the Medical Institute of Georgia. Four years later the school was renamed the Medical College of Georgia. In 1834, paperwork was signed to begin construction on a new building to house the school. Charles Cluskey was hired to work on the project. Building began and completion of the school was celebrated in 1835. A Greek Revival design was used in the masterpiece leaving a lasting impression. It would become an institution bringing forth-new medical techniques, along with Dr. Milton Anthony establishing new procedures in the field of medicine. Authorities in medicine can boast the school has produced some of the most influential doctors in the country, both past and present, but the past can come back to haunt those who keep secrets.

The Medical College of Georgia bought Gradison Harris, a Gullah slave, in 1852. Gradison was unaware of his duties until he reached Augusta. The staff schooled him in reading, writing, and anatomy. He was instructed of his position under the administrators, and began to feed their morbid desires. After reading the daily obituaries, Gradison would silently enter Cedar Grove Cemetery under the cover of darkness and begin digging. Once a coffin was reached, the top was broken open, and the body pulled out. Placing the body inside a bag, Gradison would return to the college where the body would be used as a test subject for students.

One evening two students, who witnessed the grave robber abduct a body from the cemetery, followed the parched thief to a bar. One of the students took the body from the sack, while the other climbed inside. When Gradison came outside, a voice from the bag wailed in an unearthly tone asking for a drink. Staring wide-eyed in surprise, he quickly left his prize sitting on the ground and ran down the street. Gradison left after the abolishment of slavery, returned sometime later, and took employment as a porter for the institution that once looked upon him as property. In 1911, he died at the age of ninety-five. Curiosity seekers can find his body buried at Cedar Grove Cemetery, the same ground he desecrated so many times during his life.

In 1989, during renovation of the former college, one hundred and fifty four bodies were uncovered from underneath the building. Bones were found in vats, along with body parts preserved in a foul liquid. This gives proof to the legend of Resurrection Man and souls that had yet to be laid to rest. On November 7, 1998, the bones that were uncovered from the Old Medical College were given a proper burial in Cedar Grove Cemetery.

Cedar Grove Cemetery is located across the street from Magnolia Cemetery, with its main entrance on Walker Street. Rich in history, Cedar Grove is host to many African-Americans who gained extraordinary ground for the black community in Augusta. In 1820, Augusta gave forty acres where slaves could be buried. One headstone dates to 1835, making it the oldest found. The first records of burials were recorded in 1840, but not until 1862 were records printed with name, age, sex, date of death, diseases, and name of owner. In 1865, the deceased were recorded and referred to as freeman. Pertinent information was finally logged after 1930.

Gambling was a favorite past time in Augusta for many of its residents, although memories of the activity have faded from the thoughts of most people. One memory floating in time gives birth to a legend of luck in Cedar Grove Cemetery. Numbers going to be used in gambling would be buried on the left side of a certain grave before game time on the following day. After sitting in the moist ground overnight, luck would follow the player and bring him good fortune.

African-Americans of Augusta can trace many ancestors in Cedar Grove. Time roams in silence bringing a peaceful air over the marred gravestones. Many of the markers are unreadable now, weathered away by sun and rain, but heritage and contributions given to the community still thrive today.

Persons of interest buried at Cedar Grove Cemetery:

James Carter, Sr. was Augusta's first African-American dentist.

R.A. Dent was the first African-American elected to Legislature.

Silas Floyd was a minister, poet, and wrote the biography of C.T. Walker.

Dr. T.W. Josey was a physician and supported many charities. T.W. Josey High School is named in his honor.

Rev. W.P, Russell started a free African-American school.

Dr. George Stoney, a physician, created the Lamer Hospital.

Amanda America Dickson was one of the richest African-American women in the United States at the time of her inheritance.

Rev. William J. White founded Augusta Baptist

Institute. This school would later become Morehouse College in Atlanta.

Charlie A. Ried, Sr. was a founder of Blount-Ried Funeral Home. His body was laid to rest in the first crypt in the cemetery.

Ezekiel Harris House

THE EZEKIEL HARRIS HOUSE

The Ezekiel Harris House is the second oldest structure in Augusta. Shown in the architecture of the house is a premier example of post-Revolutionary construction. When the house was completed, it featured a vaulted, arched hallway. Atop the house is a gambrel roof. As a visitor views the house from the street, tiered piazzas can be seen supported by wooden posts. Two brick chimneys, one on either side of the house, rise to the top of the three-story building. A stairway in the back of the house provides the only means of entry onto the second and third floors.

Ezekiel Harris came to Augusta in 1797 from South Carolina. He was a wealthy tobacco merchant with the idea of establishing a town that could compete with Augusta. The town he envisioned was to be called Harrisburg. Here Ezekiel wanted to build a tobacco inspection station and warehouse. Construction began on accommodations for the tobacco planters that would visit Harrisburg. Merchants would receive free lodging at the new inn and find the host willing to accommodate their every need.

The Ezekiel Harris House has been called "The White House" and "The Mackay House" in days gone by. For many years the house was thought to be the Old Mackay Trading Post where a battle occurred during the

Revolutionary War. This theory was disputed in 1975. During the dispute, evidence was found that the original site of the battle occurred somewhere across the street from the house.

Colonists were fighting for their independence from England, and in the fall of September 1780, Colonel Thomas Brown, loyalists, and a group of Cherokee Indians were holding the McKay Trading Post. Elijah Clark, and patriots of the cause, engaged the British in battle. Fighting was intense with several hundred men on either side. Colonel Brown dug in deep around the post, even though Clark had cut off all water supplies. Colonel Brown and his weakening men became overwhelmed with thirst, and had to drink urine. Hunger came and the men ate what little food they had, which only consisted of seasoned pumpkins. Colonel Brown was at the point of surrender from the relentless patriots. The weary commander thought of his past victories, he was a dedicated man of the Crown. Hearing the sounds of reinforcements, led by British Colonel Cruger, Brown regained his composure and readied his men for victory. With the introduction of more men and munitions, the loyalists were ready to renew their fight. Clark retreated from the trading post leaving twenty-nine men behind. Brown ordered the hanging of thirteen patriots, while the remaining sixteen were turned over to the Cherokee Indians to be tortured to death. Brown lay in his bed wounded with injuries he had received from gunfire during the battle. Witnessing the execution of the prisoners would not be denied Brown; he had his bed positioned so he could watch the proceedings. Early historians would later state the patriots turned over to the Indians were tortured with such ruthlessness it could not be written and recorded in print.

Augustans believe that there are strange events taking

place at the Ezekiel Harris House. Local legend tells of a ghost being seen on the property. One story that has been retold for generations is that of a woman being seen on the second and third floors of the house. A lonely figure passes room to room searching for something. Local residents believe it is the mother of two patriot brothers that were hung at the trading post. The mother was so grief stricken after receiving the news she still searches frantically for her sons that died over two hundred years ago.

Others report hearing swinging ropes tied to the stairway railings holding the heavy weight of the dead patriots. Many people say they have felt the strain of a rope around their neck as they approach the house. The creaking of the thirteenth step of the stairway sometimes screams with the cries of the doomed patriots.

Although the original area where the patriots were put to death is known today, it could be their screams from the past inhabit the only place close to where they died. Perhaps the figure of the lonely woman is the mother of the two brothers that were hung near the site, still searching, still grieving for her beloved sons.

Bellevue

BELLEVUE

Bellevue, the name flows with an elegant grace. Translation of the name means Beautiful Vista. Freeman Walker, a mayor of Augusta and U.S. Senator, built the house around 1805. The area where he chose to build Bellevue was a section of town known as "The Hill". It was a popular place where summer homes were built. Bellevue is an example of a Sands Hill cottage, a popular style of architecture for summer homes.

The Augusta Arsenal once stood on the Savannah River occupied by a garrison of men. Swamp fever, a dreaded disease, reared itself taking the lives of most of the inhabitants. Captain Matthew Payne was in command of the arsenal when the swampy marsh released its deadly curse. Recanted stories from the past suggest Captain Payne would have fallen to the effects of swamp fever, had he not been visiting Freeman Walker at Bellevue. Having regained his health, Payne brought to the attention of the government that the Hill section of Augusta on Walton Way would prove to be healthier than the marshy Savannah site. So began the construction of the Augusta Arsenal at Bellevue.

Government orders brought 22,000 muskets and rifles to the arsenal. Captain Arnold Elzey was sent by the federal government to secure the arms. Born in 1816, Elzey was a graduate of West Point. The arsenal was surrendered in

January of 1861 to Confederate troops led by Colonel W.H. Walker. Resigning his commission, Elzey joined Confederate service, and received promotion to the rank of Colonel.

Tradition states the Galt family lived in Bellevue around 1861. John Galt kept residence in the house with his two daughters, Emily and Lucy. Relations between the North and South were growing bitter, Lincoln winning the presidential election was a blow to the South, and talk of secession permeated the minds of the community.

Emily met a young solider at the Arsenal, the two fell in love, and it was not long before they were engaged to be married. The ring the handsome Confederate gave to her was as magnificent as any diamond her innocent eyes had seen before. She would often look at the diamond ring that adorned her delicate finger. One day, while in a room on the second floor of the house, she took the ring from her finger. Emily began to slowly engrave her name onto the pane of glass in the window. Lucy stood watching, took the ring from her sister, and carved her name next to Emily's. The date 1861 stands next to the names to forever authenticate their work. Emily's fiancé joined the Confederate cause, and died in battle. She had dreamed of the perfect day in her life, when she and her beloved would be married. Burdened with a grieving heart she flung herself from the same second story window on which she had etched her name.

According to an employee in the counseling and testing center of Augusta State University strange occurrences have been noted inside of Bellevue. The employee states that although nothing has happened to her, two of her co-workers have spoken of unusual happenings. The first incident was with her predecessor. Staying later than usual the employee heard two people arguing in the hallway. Getting up from her chair, peering down the hallway, she found it empty. A second incident occurred when another woman stayed late. Again two voices were heard coming from the hallway, and when she checked no one was there. Counselors theorize that the voices are the arguments of Emily and her fiancé fighting about him going off to war.

Eyes have wandered and searched the hallways of Bellevue and have been unable to find the source of the disturbance. When silence descends upon the house after employees leave, a voice or two continues the disagreement chiseled in time over a century ago.

Outraged, Emily continues to voice her displeasure with the decision made by the young solider. Feeling that the sons of the southern states must gather to confront a common enemy in the North, he pled his case in earnest to Emily. Determined destiny had set events in motion, he bravely went to fight a cause that meant more to him than the woman he loved.

Benet House

THE BENET HOUSE

Built between 1827 and 1829, the Benet House is currently home to the admissions office of Augusta State University. Tuscan pillars support a two-tiered portico. Going through many changes during the nineteenth and twentieth centuries, the house maintains its ageless image with an exceptional grace. Many presidents of the university have used the house as primary living quarters.

Stephan Vincent Benet, Pulitzer Prize winner, lived at the Arsenal with his father who was one of the early commanders of the government property. Vincent was born July 22, 1898, and hailed from Bethlehem, Pennsylvania. He penned words lovingly until his death on March 19, 1943. During his life Stephan offered the world literary wonder when facing uncertain times and joyous occasions.

Standing tall and branching forth in celebration of life, a lone oak secures a legend from the past. There is a brick walkway leading to the oak and a bench where students can spend time in conversation. Underneath the gaze of the tree, Stephan Benet concentrated on his studies, enjoying the shade produced by the wide branches and many leaves.

Legend tells of an early commander stationed at the Augusta Arsenal. He was married to a stately woman of the time. Enthralled with the finest clothes available, the southern belle spent hours admiring the expensive garments hanging in the closet. She insisted the maid bring morning tea to the upstairs bedroom, so she could drink in front of a mirror. Hunting was a second passion of the commandant; many days would pass with the enjoyment of the outdoor sport on his mind. Leaving the house before daybreak was not uncommon for the commander. One morning, as was custom, the maid brought tea to the mistress of the house. When the maid entered the room she found the mistress dead on the floor with a tea tray beside her. According to the commander, he had brought tea to his wife that morning before he left for the hunt. Accusations were made of murder, but no conviction would stand against him.

Another legend passed down through time is that of a commander sent to the Augusta Arsenal after the Civil War during the Reconstruction. The commander hired his nephew to work for two dollars a day. People became jealous of the pay being received by the young man, and envy set upon them. Leaving work one day to get a piece of apple pie, the commander's nephew was shot and killed on the steps of the house by someone hiding nearby.

Employees and students staying a little later than usual hear strange noises coming from the kitchen area of the house. Stories contribute the occurrences to the young man searching the kitchen cabinets for apple pie.

Nervous feelings shudder even the most leathered skinned personality when left alone in late hours after nightfall in the darkened rooms surrounding fragile flesh and bone. Clothes sometimes swagger back and forth inside of the upstairs closet where the mistress from so long ago admires her new acquisitions. Seeking the appropriate dress for the trial in which her husband would attend to determine his innocence. Perhaps foul play did befall the mistress and she seeks the one who caused her demise, whether it is her husband or another hidden in the annals of time.

Look to the kitchen when a gourmet pie is cooked

because the commander's nephew still craves his favorite dish to fill his famished stomach. A startled cook may find an unwanted guest lurking around the corner.

Walker Cemetery

CONFEDERATE GHOST

reeman Walker was born in Charles City, Virginia on October 25, 1780. In 1797, the decision to move to Augusta was made where he studied law and began to practice his craft. He is remembered as a handsome southern gentleman with quick wit. Career decisions prompted him to become one of Augusta's most successful sons. During his life he was elected to the Georgia State Legislature and the United States Senate, and was a mayor of Augusta. He also owned the land where Augusta State University now resides. Before the university came, the property was called the Augusta Arsenal. Walker sold the property to the United States government where the land received the name so familiar to many Augustans. The former owner was allowed to keep a small piece of land to use as a cemetery. Between the original house used by former commanders and buildings that served through many wars, along with the Walker Cemetery, Augusta State University holds together fine twines of history that are interwoven to provide all people with a view into yesteryear.

The cemetery is shrouded by trees protecting the gravestones with their overhanging limbs, sunlight penetrates only slightly. Erosion has tried with failed attempts to defame the words set into the stonework. Today the graveyard is still used by the Walker family. They have kept alive the history of the cemetery with its continued use, and set in position a marker for important Augustans of the past.

There is an interesting story involving the cemetery that is known to many students and staff at the college. One night a professor from the college stayed late to help a student. When the two finished, they parted ways, each ready to go home. Looking across campus, the professor observed what he thought to be a student walking. It seemed odd to the professor for a student to be out wandering the grounds at such an hour, especially in the strange outfit clothing his body. Continuing to walk, the figure finally stopped at the cemetery. It seemed the student vanished behind some trees, but that would be impossible because the college placed wire around that particular area. Considering the circumstances, the only plausible way to pass through the wire would be to step over it or crawl under it, neither of which happened. Early the next morning, after intense investigation, the professor realized the clothing worn by the figure was a Confederate uniform.

Inside the iron fence surrounding the Walker Cemetery there lie the remains of Confederate soldiers who fought for a cause they believed in. The figure seen walking the grounds in the early evening hours may be searching areas of Augusta State University where the Augusta Arsenal once stood, visiting old buildings still standing and attempting to protect the cause he once fought for.

Sibley Mill

WOMAN IN THE WEAVING ROOM

Sibley Mill is located on Goodrich Street off Broad Street in downtown Augusta. People also know the site as the location where the Confederate Powder Works once stood, producing tons of gunpowder for Confederate soldiers to utilize against the North during the Civil War.

George Washington Rains was ordered to look throughout the South for a suitable place to build a factory that would produce gunpowder for the protection of the Confederate States. He suggested the railroads, Savannah River, and the Augusta Canal would provide effective waterpower and transportation for the product, so construction began on a building to produce it.

When the powderworks was finished it stretched for two miles and was the primary producer of gunpowder in the South. The gunpowder produced at the time was considered to be of the highest quality and was given recognition in the defense of Charleston, South Carolina. During the time it was in operation, until April 18, 1865, the powderworks made 2,750,000 pounds of gunpowder. Women of Augusta participated in the war effort, producing some 75,000 cartridges in a single day. After the war the powderworks was dismantled with a single chimney being left on the site as a memorial to the building that once stood there.

In 1880, the Sibley Mill, named for Josiah Sibley, was built around the remaining chimney from the powderworks. The building was modeled after England's Parliament House and shows some Romanesque influence. High atop the grand building architectural feats exhibit beautiful battlements, decorated towers, and parapets reminiscent of medieval castles.

Waterpower is an important source of energy in the daily operations of the Sibley Mill. Sixty percent of its power comes from the canal with the other forty percent being supplied by Georgia Power. It is easy to see the importance of the canal when looking at the mill sitting next to it. Most of the time all is peaceful except the sounds of passing cars and machinery in operation, but this was not the case on October 20, 1906.

Tragedy struck one quiet morning as workers tended to their weaving machines with supervisors watching with careful eyes the progress of the workers efforts. As one of the workers, a woman named Maude Williams, was earning her wage, an irate man named Arthur Glover entered the room. The mood of the room changed from business-as-usual to fear when he pointed a gun at the unsuspecting victim, fired a shot, and killed the woman.

Later it was found that Maude was secretly having an affair with the man, who was married, and decided to break off the relationship causing him to lose his mind.

Sibley Mill
and site of
the Confederate Powderworks

Justice came in the form of hanging after sentence was passed on him for murder.

After the violent death of Maude Williams, workers weaving in the same room where she was killed claim to have seen her ghost. People walking through the room when it should be empty have seen a lone woman working intently at the weaving machine, ignoring the newcomer. Sometimes workers recognized the figure as Maude Williams and ran with fright into inner the most part of the building. New employees attempted to talk to the busy woman, but would receive no reply. Each time it was reported, the weaving machine was in complete operation and running, when the room should have been empty and the machine turned off.

Sibley Mill is still in operation today, serving an important role in Augusta's economy by the products made there and people it employs. There have been no reports of people seeing Maude Williams for many years; at least none of which are spoken of in public. Perhaps she weaves somewhere else now; content that justice was served in her name.

Nicholas Ware House

THE NICHOLAS WARE HOUSE

t has been called one of the finest examples of Federal architecture in the south and was once thought to be an incredible waste of money at the cost of forty thousand dollars when it was built in 1818. On the corner of Greene and Fifth Street stands the home of Nicholas Ware. People began to call the house "Ware's Folly" because of the large sum of money that was employed for its construction.

Nicholas Ware came to Augusta from Virginia when he was a child. Later in life he became the Mayor of Augusta and served in the Georgia Legislature. He served as a United States Senator where he died in office.

There are four levels to the building, including a basement. Outside matching two-story bays flank a bowed two-story portico on the front and back of the house. The interior staircases, along with the outside stairs dominate the structure with an awe-inspiring view. It is believed that Gabriel Manigault built the house.

Many memorable occasions have occurred in the house, which Augustans hold close to their hearts. When the Marquis de LaFayette visited Augusta in 1825, he was given a ball in his honor at the house and danced the minuet. Another event was when Emily Tubman, a generous philanthropist, met Richard Tubman while visiting the Nicholas Ware home on winter vacation. They were soon married and shared a wonderful life together. After his death she became a contributor to many buildings constructed in the Augusta area and was the founder of several local organizations.

Many prominent Augusta families have lived in the house over the years. Birth and death have been companions to those living in the house over the past two centuries, giving way to someone not willing to leave their beloved home. Looking back, Augustans reflect on stories of unexplained occurrences inside of the house with new ones emerging all the time.

Listen quietly when alone and see what can be heard around you. People tell stories of ghosts lingering and claim to have heard footsteps on the upstairs floors. They are distinctive footsteps, heel to toe, walking across the wooden floors. One unique place for the activity is on the top floor where there was once a nursery. A number of sounds have been heard in the room, but when checked there was no one there. Whenever any floor was searched after the footsteps were heard, the house was empty.

Another strange occurrence people have experienced is the doorbell ringing. When the door is answered, there is nothing but empty space behind the closed entranceway. The wiring to the doorbell has been checked by professionals and found to be in order, but after they leave the ringing starts again.

Probably the most exciting phenomenon that has happened to someone in the building is the feeling of a presence. Whether it is a feeling that someone is there or a cold spot, something lingers in the hallways and has no intention on leaving. In the past an employee at the art center has felt the brush of something against her face, but again the room was empty.

In 1935, when the house was being renovated a work

crew found bones inside a wall on the first floor. They did not know at the time the bones would be later identified as human. Soon a young lady came forward and admitted she knew where the bones had come from. She told the story of when she was a child and lived in the house with her family.

Behind the house was a garden filled with beautiful flowers which bloomed in any season no matter how hot or cold it was. One activity she enjoyed was playing in the garden amongst the flowers digging in the moist dirt. She only did this when her mother was gone because she knew of her mother's disapproval.

One day after her mother had left she went into the garden and began digging. She removed a sufficient amount of dirt and a small hole began to form. When the little girl looked down she observed with curiosity several solid white pieces of what appeared to be rocks. Only after picking the pieces up did she realize the rocks were really bones.

She took the bones into the house trying to decide what to do with the new found objects. As far as she knew the pieces of material she held were nothing more than animal bone. A little while later she walked to the attic at the top of the house and began to play. It wasn't long after the door slammed and her mother declared her presence. Scared at what action her mother might take if she found out there had been digging in the garden, the little girl dropped the bones through a hole near the attic ceiling. The bones fell to the first floor and remained in the wall until they were found years later. To this day it is unknown who the bones belong to or why they were buried in the garden.

There has not been a physical sighting reported in the house, at least none known at the present time, but there is said to be a friendly spirit, sometimes comical, dwelling in the hallways and rooms. Families living in the house in the past have reported hearing strange noises and tell of a spirit being present. Who the ghost is may be anyone's guess for many people have lived and died in the home. If you are visiting the house for an activity listen quietly for footsteps or a doorbell ringing, there may just be someone waiting to meet you.

Old Craig Houghton School

CRAIG HOUGHTON SCHOOL

When John Houghton moved to Augusta he could have never known the impact he would leave on the city that has lasted even until today. He had a brilliant mind and ventured into business in the downtown area. Eventually his business decisions became fruitful and soon great wealth was amassed. John Houghton died in 1851 leaving a grieving city behind. A considerable sum of money was left to Augusta to build a school and name it after him. One condition was that children could attend free. Soon after his death, a new school opened its doors to the public bearing the Houghton name.

Fire ravaged downtown Augusta in 1916, leaving the city decimated. The Houghton School fell to its knees as an unwilling disciple of the inferno. Recovery revived the community, and a new school was built in 1917. Lloyd Preacher was hired as the architect. Construction cost bore upwards of sixty thousand dollars, making the school far more expensive than its predecessor. Spanish Colonial revival sets the mood of a beautiful architectural design.

During daylight hours nothing seems unique about the school sitting on Broad Street. Nightfall releases shadows that envelop the white brick building. Darkness falls onto the iron gates protecting the entrance where Houghton's body lay in silence. Passing cars illuminate the borders of the school with low beam lights giving reflection from rows of dusty windows. Large trees stand at attention near the main entrance offering suggestive reasons of why not to approach the exterior. When the doors close behind the parents coming to pick up children, echoes can be heard chiming over and over throughout the school causing the hair to rise on the back of their necks. Maybe the echoes can be compared to the footsteps of John Houghton checking his namesake to make certain the orders from his will were carried forth.

Teachers and students adhere to strong beliefs that a presence ventures into the hallways when all becomes quiet. Shadows and echoes become one, combining questions of uncertainty of what may rest around the corner. Although most employees and students disregard suspicious activity, there are people that have told stories over the years.

Children tell each other a generations old story of Houghton pushing students down the stairwell. Loud bangs and creaks are often heard and are unexplainable. Shadowy figures flash before their unbelieving eyes and suddenly disappear.

In December of 2000, the Houghton School was closed. A new school was built on Fourth at Hale Street and was rededicated to the man who loved Augusta with his heart and soul. John Houghton may walk the halls of the vacant school, keeping an eye on happenings perking his interest. Even when occupied, he would no doubt look after children attending daily classes. Pushing them down stairs would not be his style.

Old Government House

THE OLD GOVERNMENT HOUSE

O nce one of the most important buildings in Augusta, the Old Government House is still recognized as a central aspect of history in the city. Many Augustans know the building as the "Old Murphy House", but before being transformed into a private residence it had a greater calling.

It can be hard to imagine the first purpose served by the house when walking the lavish grounds. Many government officials have passed through the doors of the house. The main purpose of the building constructed in 1801 was to house the headquarters and seat of Augusta's city government. It is thought Gabriel Manigault, an architect from Charleston, South Carolina, designed the building.

Represented in the house is a palette of designs giving way to an impression of several architectural feats. A Federal design was the foundation of the original work, including brick parapet walls and tall chimneys on either side of the building. Later the exterior was finished in stucco. An iron portico and balcony, along with new window trim, finished the reflection of Regency style architecture. In later years, parts of the interior were remolded in a Greek Revival style. There is absolute beauty compiled from the years of changes outside and inside of the house.

Many great figures from Augusta's history have lived inside the whispering walls of the home. Mayor Samuel Hale purchased the building in 1821, and began the necessary steps to make it into a home. Massilon Stovall is another notable Augustan who lived in the house, and would later have a street named after him.

One of the longest residing families of the Government House is the Murphy family. In 1877, Dr. Edmund T. Murphy bought the house and lived here for seventy-five years. After his death, the Murphy family lived in the home for only a short while. Throughout the years the house has shook hands with many owners, and would eventually be bought by the city of Augusta from the Junior League.

Inside the house many antique paintings decorate the walls giving remembrance to owners and caretakers of the timeless structure. Mirrors beautified in gold were brought from France by Fitzemmens, a former resident, stretch from the ceiling to the floor with a magnificent width arresting images from the past in eternal reflection. To accompany the mirrors are cornices with the same intricate details.

When Georgia Washington visited Augusta in 1791, he ate dinner with Governor Telfair and other prominent officials late in the evening on the day he arrived. There were several toasts given in the president's honor that evening. Later he visited Richmond Academy and expressed great satisfaction with the performance of its students.

Representatives of the city gave the president a grand tour of Augusta, showing off future places and plans of development. A ginkgo tree is planted outside of the house next to a roadway made of stone. Legend says the tree was planted in honor of George Washington's visit to Augusta and grows where his feet had trod that historic day. It lists as the largest ginkgo tree in Georgia and second largest in the United States with over a thirteen-foot circumference.

Reaching for the heavens, branches stretch eighty feet into the sky with a crown topping seventy feet.

Springtime reveals beautiful gardens surrounding the house with vegetation looking almost prehistoric. A two hundred-year-old crepe myrtle stands next to huge oak trees that were planted in true Southern fashion. Truly there are no gardens in the city that can rival the artistic beauty given to the landscape.

Beside the house winds a stone roadway that once clicked with the sounds of horse-drawn carriages. Legend says the stones were taken from the bottom of a ship. They were kept there to keep the vessels from rocking back and forth during its voyage.

One eerie story has been handed down through generations of Augustans. On the second story of the building, in a room where silence can overtake the conscious, a clock used to sit winding down time with its pointed hands. Without fail, chimes would echo throughout the house to alert the occupants to the top of the hour. Every morning when someone would go to wind the clock, it had already been done. The clock was said to have wound itself over and over again every night.

Look west down Telfair Street and the Brahe House, known as the first house in Augusta to be wired for electricity, can be seen several yards away on the same side of the street. The house was built about 1850 and is an excellent piece of architecture known as a Sands Hill Cottage. Fredrick Brahe moved to Augusta from the northern part of the United States and took occupation as a silversmith. He was also the Official Tender of the City Clock, taking enormous pride in the job of keeping Augusta on time. Even though he was a keeper of time, he could not prevent the inevitable and died when old age overtook his body.

Not long after the clock was found to be mysteriously

winding itself did the residing family come to the conclusion that perhaps Brahe's ghost was making daily rounds winding the clock on the second floor. He always kept the people of Augusta attuned to the exact time before climbing down from the old mechanism. It was only reasonable since the clock he attended no longer existed that he find another to lovingly watch and tend to.

Today the house plays host to weddings, parties, Christmas and New Year's Eve gala, and social events. There rest an important role in the building that once heard the sound of pounding gavels and justifiable sentencing of judicial cases. Untouched by the hands of time, the building is recognized as one of the legendary aspects of Augusta's development.

When George Washington arrived in Augusta he had dinner late in the afternoon with the governor and other officials. The men held their glasses high and made fifteen toasts on that historic day. On May 21, 1791, the *Augusta Chronicle* reported toasts were made to the following:

The United States
The State of Georgia
The joyful occasion
The Vice-President
The Fourth of July
        The 17th of October, 1777
        The 19th of October, 1781
        The memory of General Greene
        Those who bravely fell in the defense of American Liberty
        Our ministers at foreign courts
Agriculture
Commerce
Arts and Science
Republican Virtue

Savannah River

WILLIAM LONGSTREET

Dreams come true for many when their ideas float in a vast sea of conjuring and invention. William Longstreet of Augusta, Georgia, rests in the arms of history as a man that fulfilled a dream, but was forgotten and pushed away from the eyes of notability. Many believe that he was the original inventor of the steamboat and has been overlooked with barely a mention in history.

William Longstreet came to Augusta soon after the Revolutionary War had ended. He was of Dutch descent and has been described as a genius with a warm heart, as well as holding traits of determination and stubbornness. His personality helped propel him, regardless of criticism by the public, to achieve his goal.

In 1787, William Longstreet built a small boat that resembled a child's toy to test his theory that steam power could propel objects on water. He found the test run to be successful and later the following year applied and received a patent from the state of Georgia.

Finally it was time to build a vessel that would prove him right, and in 1807 he held the first demonstration of the watercraft by launching it and traveling down the Savannah River. Many people doubted the safety of the boat, including his friends, but after continuous convincing he found a few brave souls to risk life and limb to travel on an old mode of transportation now powered by steam. Waters divided as the front of the vessel broke waves gathered up from the Savannah River. Standing on the bank along the river people clapped and cheered in disbelief while William Longstreet smiled at his success.

Only a few days prior did Robert Fulton launch his steamboat, the Clermont, and completed a successful run. He was noted as the inventor of the steamboat, but William Longstreet is recorded as the first to use the idea, and despite debate was the first to employ the theory of powering a boat on water by using steam power.

His idea was to place poles together attached to an arm and when the arm rotated the poles would push against the bottom of the body of water on which the boat was traveling to propel it in the direction desired by the operator. Along with the shrewd moving components, the entire mechanism was powered by steam.

In the years following Eli Whitney's invention of the cotton gin, Longstreet saw another potential for using steam and created a steam-powered cotton gin. It is recorded by the Longstreet Society that he owned mills in Augusta and St. Mary's, Georgia, which were burned by the British in the War of 1812. Fate seemed to give favor to him and just as quickly take parts of his success from him.

During the tumultuous time William Longstreet struggled with his invention he sought help from another source. On September 26, 1790 he wrote to Edward Ellis about his idea. Recorded in the Georgia Archives is the following letter:

> Sir, I make no doubt but you have often heard of my steamboat and as often heard it laughed at. But in this I have only shared the fate of all other projectors, for it has uniformly been the custom of every country to ridicule

even the greatest inventions until use has proven their utility.

In not reducing my scheme to practice has been unfortunate for me, I confess, and perhaps for the people in general, but until very lately I did not think that artists or material could be had in the place sufficient. However, necessity, that grand science of invention, has furnished me with an idea of perfecting my plans almost entirely of wooden material, and by such workmen as may be got here, and from a through confidence of its success, I have presumed to ask your assistance and patronage. Should it succeed agreeably to my expectations, I hope I shall discover that source of duty which such favors always merit, and should it not succeed, your reward must lay with other unlucky adventures.

For me to mention all of the advantages arising from such a machine would be tedious, and, indeed, quite unnecessary. Therefore I have taken the liberty to state in this plain and humble manner, my wish and opinion, which I hope you will excuse, and I shall remain, either with or without approbation,

Your Excellency's most obedient and humble servant,

William Longstreet

Lost in time a story rests from long ago of an Augustan having witnessed something unbelievable while standing on the banks of the Savannah River early one morning. Dawn was about to break and the time for fishing on this day was perfect. So down to the muddy bank of the river the old man went to set his fishing pole not knowing he was about to encounter a presence from the past.

This particular morning a fog had rolled over the dark waters that engulfed the fishing line thrown out into the river. It wasn't long before the old man sensed a fish about to strike. He snatched the pole toward his body to set the hook when all of a sudden he saw a boat emerging from the fog. Slowly the boat traveled past him being propelled by steam.

One the deck of the boat the old man watched as men worked quickly to keep whatever job they were assigned in order. Several times a lone man on one end of the vessel would yell the name William.

William Longstreet stands as a great man and legend in Georgia for his contributions to the world. He could not have known that one day the inventions his brilliant mind conjured would impact his community and the people around him. Robert Fulton did create a steamboat that traveled through water using paddle wheels, but the credit of invention goes to William Longstreet for being the first to move a boat by steam power.

Tomb of Wylly Barron

MAGNOLIA CEMETERY

Strolling through Magnolia Cemetery, underneath four hundred flowering trees the mind fades back through history. Sculptured statues make up this marble and concrete city. The brick walkways are similar to the yellow brick road from *"Wizard of OZ"*, taking the visitor on mysterious adventures. Surrounding the cemetery is a red brick wall encompassing sixty acres. Inside the main office records abound with written testimony of the past. The eastside of the wall was fortified to protect Augusta during the Civil War. In 1817, the de Laigle family, who owned the property, gave it to the city of Augusta.

Magnolia Cemetery began its inurn of the dead with the burial of J.Hartford Montgomery on December 24, 1800, although the first official burial was in August of 1818. Hosting resting places of Confederate and Union soldiers, seven Confederate Generals, governors of Georgia, and mayors of Augusta, the cemetery is rich in history. Magnolia hosts the burial site of James Ryder Randall, author of "Maryland, My Maryland", who was a literary genius.

One legend that seeps from a mausoleum in the cemetery is that of Wylly Barron, a wealthy prominent man, who owned the Atkinson Hotel. Inside the building, patrons could gamble and drink all day if they wanted. A gambler, who lost all his money and later took his own life, issued a curse upon Barron. The gambler said," You have taken everything I have. When you die, may you not have even a grave to shelter you!"

Time progressed and Barron became very superstitious about the prospects of gambling. Rules were made in the hotel as to who could gamble. If a man's employment meant he handled large sums of money or the wage he was paid was insufficient, then he was not allowed to participate in the activities. Monetary contributions to charities were made in secret. Frightened what the future might hold, he built a granite mausoleum in 1870, twenty-four years before his death.

Winter of his life finally arrived, and Barron died at the age of eighty-eight. Because he lost his entire fortune before his death, there was not enough money in the estate to purchase a coffin, so bricks were used to encase his body. In compliance with Barron's last will and testament the mausoleum's keyhole was sealed, and the key thrown into the Savannah River.

In 1875, the last person to die in a duel at Sand Bar Ferry was Charles Tilly. Tilly was attempting to defend the honor of one of the de Laigle daughters. During the duel he was shot and killed. Showing bravery by defending the family's honor, the de Laigle family buried him in their cemetery.

Men do not make history, history makes men. History is preserved forever in the stonework resting beside the people who founded and built Augusta. Many years ago people would come to the cemetery carrying a picnic, along with the family. Children running and playing among the gravestones was not an uncommon activity in the early 1900's. Time spent with past family members was considered a healing and joyous occasion. Now the responsibility for remembrance falls on the shoulders of visitors, historians, and keepers of the cemetery grounds.

Confederate Dead at Magnolia Cemetery

Confederate cemetery section of Magnolia
Cemetery with unexplained orbs seen in the
photograph.

Civil War Generals buried at Magnolia cemetery.
General Bryan Goode
General William D. Smith
General Marcellus A. Stovall
Brig. General Victor Jean Batiste Girardy
Brig. General John K. Jackson
Brig. General Edward P. Alexander
Major General Ambrose R. Wright

Other people of interest buried at Magnolia Cemetery.

General George Evans, served as a mayor of Augusta.

General Thomas Glascock, served in the War of 1812 and Seminole War of 1817.

Paul Hamilton Hayne, Southern poet of the 19th century.

William White, served as a mayor of Augusta. He was an officer in the War of 1812.

de Laigle House

GHOST OF CHARLES TILLY

Across from the street from the Augusta-Richmond County Municipal building sits an Italianate style building that was once home to the de Laigle family of Augusta. The house is made of brick and is covered with a pale blue stucco. Often called the "*Addams Family House*" by Augustans because of its resemblance to the house in the old television show *The Addams Family*, the house was built in 1873 and purchased by the city of Augusta to serve as the District Attorney's office. In 2002, the city proposed to demolish the building to use as a parking lot, but was soon saved by the outraged citizens and family members of the de Laigle Family.

The de Laigle family contributed much to Augusta in its earlier years, and is most noted for giving the city the land where Magnolia Cemetery sits. In the 1940's a descendant of the de Laigle family contributed monies to the cemetery to build the Sexton's Lodge. Another noted fact is that the de Laigle family owned the first brick manufacturing company in the south, becoming a strong support for the local economy.

There is a tragic story that fills the walls of the de Laigle House and that is of a man named Charles Dawson Tilly. Charles Tilly was born in Ireland and migrated to Georgia.

He decided to settle in Augusta not long after his

arrival. He soon met the generous members of the de Laigle family and was offered a room in the basement that he could rent for a small fee. Shortly thereafter Tilly and the de Laigles became close friends.

One day a man named George Ratcliffe made the remark that Tilly and Mary de Laigle were having an affair. This accusation made Tilly furious and the red tempered Irishman challenged Ratcliffe to a duel on the Sand Bar Ferry. Dueling had been outlawed in Georgia many years earlier, but this did not stop people from using the age-old custom to help defend and maintain their honor. There was no way Ratcliffe was going to get away with such a statement, and the de Laigle's honor was not about to be blemished.

Early the next day the two men met on the Sand Bar Ferry, the site of numerous duels, with their seconds. Each man readied their pistols, stood back to back, and walked the required steps from each other in opposite directions. When the final step was counted, both men turned and fired. Ratcliffe's aim was true, and the bullet from his weapon struck Tilly, leaving a mortal wound. Tilly was taken by his second back to his room in the basement of the de Laigle House, where he died the next day in the company of his beloved friends, on December 17, 1875.

Ironically, this was the last duel to be fought on the Sand Bar Ferry and the last to be fought in Georgia. Citizens considered the death of the young man a tragedy, and came in droves to pay their respects. The story also gained national attention where it was printed in newspapers across the country.

Because of his great bravery and attempts to protect Mary de Laigle's honor, Charles Tilly was laid to rest among the members of the de Laigle family. A portrait of Tilly can be found hanging inside the building that serves as offices for Magnolia Cemetery. The inscription on his memorial reads as follows:

"Here lyeth the body of Charles Tilly, born in Ireland 1845, died in Augusta 1875. Glorious in youth and beauty, gallant and brave, Charles Dawson Tilly, a young Irishman, was tragically killed in the last duel fought at Sand Bar Ferry."

According to stories of people that have lived in the building when it was a home and later an office building, Charles Tilly still walks the halls and can be heard in the basement of the house. Footsteps walking down stairs, moaning, and cold spots spur many a nonbeliever to accept the fact that someone is present. Many have given accounts of feeling a presence that seems to be unhappy, not angry, but possibly sad.

Could it be there was a secret relationship between Mary de Laigle and Charles Tilly? There are people who believe there was love affair between the two. On any given afternoon when the hour becomes late or darkness has fallen, someone alone can hear Tilly walking, possibly searching for a love from long ago. If there were an affair, the proof has been kept in the past. Maybe Tilly is searching for the family that became some of his dearest friends or cannot accept the death that was so tragic. Whichever may be the reason, the spirit of a man not at peace roams the hallways of one of Augusta's most beloved buildings.

The following letter was written to *The Augusta Chronicle* about the de Laigle house and the importance of preserving history.

There is so much history in Augusta that goes unnoticed. The de Laigle family gave much to Augusta, with the most noted being the land for Magnolia Cemetery. Not only is the building sitting across from the Municipal

Building historic, it holds wondrous stories that have been shared among locals for years.

The house is the place where Charles Tilly, the last man to die in a duel on the Sand Bar Ferry, lived with the de Laigle family. He was taken back to the home where he stayed with the family whose honor he was trying to protect and died in their company.

His story is tragic, just as the outcome of this building will be if Augusta does not protect its history and legacy. Augusta needs to progress with new additions and buildings being erected, but preservation must come to the forefront, just as modern progress has. The building can be preserved. The Old Government House is owned by the city and is used in a very educational and favorable manner. It is one of the most important sites in Augusta where history is concerned, just as the de Laigle house is.

These places can be torn down to build parking lots, but when they are gone, they are gone, and there is no bringing them back. Augusta is Georgia's second oldest city, and when historic buildings are gone, there is nobody to see what we were and what we have become. They are unable to see the memory lane and walk down avenues of Augusta's past. So look around and see what great losses we will amass if we continue to destroy our history.

Sean Joiner-Augusta

Old Woman and the Witch

THE OLD WOMAN AND THE WITCH

A story that has been passed down through generations of the African-American community is the story of an elderly woman that rode a broom with a witch at night. The story dates back to the slave period in Augusta and arrested the imagination of the community over the years.

Late at night when the moon shone in its brilliance and the sky was clear a witch would come to the window of an elderly slave woman and knock on the window of her house. She was never startled when the witch arrived and was rather fond of her. Looking over next to her to make certain her husband was asleep, the old woman got up from bed and went into the kitchen. There she placed a washtub on the floor, stood inside the large metal pan, and pulled the skin from her body, appearing as an unholy serpent shedding its scales.

She stepped from the washtub with moonlight illuminating the muscles and veins exposed from the absence of her skin. The old woman lifted herself from the ground using a magic spell, then flew from the kitchen window onto a broomstick occupied by the witch and took off riding the dark skies all night.

When the woman arrived home in the early morning hours she stepped back into the washtub and said to the skin, "Skinny, Skinny don't you know me?" Seconds after the words were spoken, the skin would reemerge with her body and she would settle back into bed until the sun broke over the horizon at daybreak.

Night after night the old woman would meet with the witch, but as luck would have it one night her husband woke from his sleep and found her gone. This pattern repeated itself and soon he decided to find out where she was going and who she was spending time with.

One night when his wife thought he was asleep she rose from the bed when the witch knocked on the window. She went into the kitchen and repeated the same routine she had so many nights before. After she had left with the witch he put salt and pepper inside of the washtub leaving the skin covered in the spices. Inside the bedroom he waited quietly for her return. Shortly before dawn he heard his wife in the kitchen repeating the rhyme over and over again.

Motionless and resistant to her charms, the skin ignored its owner. The skinless figure began screaming for the witch. When the witch arrived, the old woman got onto the broomstick with her companion and flew away never to be seen or heard from again.

Cedar Grove

CEDAR GROVE PLANTATION

Benjamin Berry was a prosperous planter from Georgia. He traveled to Virginia where he met and married Emily Alexander. The city of Alexandria, Virginia, was named after her. Arriving back in Georgia many years later, Benjamin purchased six hundred and ninety-six acres of land where he built Cedar Grove Plantation. After building the beautiful house, he planted cedar trees to enhance the magnificence and beauty of the property. Sometime during the Civil War, Benjamin died. Widowed and seeking advantageous companionship for the property and her well being, Emily decided to marry Confederate General George W. Evans. Before consummation of the marriage, the general agreed to sign away all rights to Emily's property, which was to be bequeathed to her descendants. The Berry family owned Cedar Grove until 1903.

John Bivens purchased the property, then awarded contract to Charles Bohler, Sr. Cedar Grove would eventually become known as the Bohler Mansion. After transferring hands several more times, Cedar Grove was bought and given to the Episcopal Church of Our Savior. Parts of the house were renovated for church activities, with the cedar trees cut down to make room for a new parish.

It wasn't long after the trees had been removed that unexplained events began to transpire inside the house. Lights have been seen moving from room to room after dark, while others have heard footsteps inside of the house.

The Smith family lived behind the property for years and several times experienced unexplained occurrences inside of their Holiday Park home. Conversations have been heard when there was no company present in the house. One account told by the homeowner occurred when a bedroom closet door was opened to attend to daily chores. All of a sudden the items sitting on the shelves inside the closet were thrown across the room by some unseen force. Footsteps have been heard walking the hallway when only one person was home. Family pets have been seen watching empty air as if in a trance while some unseen spirit moved through a room.

Mr. Smith theorizes that part of the neighborhood was built on top of a graveyard that had been used by the owners of Cedar Grove in its early years. Reasoning behind the theory comes from the time he was digging holes in the yard for a new fence. Looking down at fresh dirt piled onto the ground from a shovel, several pieces of calcified bone were found at different intervals in the yard.

Over the years, people have concluded the presence lurking within the plantation house to be that of Benjamin Berry or General Evans. Sleep must have befell whichever spirit dwells on the site, for all has been quiet upon the grounds that once permeated the circular drive with the grandeur of cedars.

Road of Doom

THE LOUISVILLE DEVIL

Not far from Augusta, winding dirt roads fill the county seat of Jefferson County, Georgia, in vein-like manner crisscrossing the county as a spider spinning its web. An old Ford Model T travels past farmhouses and fields white with cotton. Blanche sits in the back seat with her sister Maggie, both breathing dust thrown into the air by car wheels. There is a lull in the air seemingly no different than any other day. Soon darkness falls onto the road as night comes to engulf the world.

Now everyone in the small town of Louisville had heard the tale of the Louisville Devil, but most paid no attention to such nonsense. The few that did believe know on any given night while traveling the dark roads, a harbinger of death could appear to warn of or appoint death to those it chose.

As the family was driving back home from business conducted in town, Blanche's father looked into the rearview mirror and saw his young daughter falling asleep, her head slumped to one side from the exhaustion of playing in the town park. A second glance caught Maggie trying to give her sister a wet willy while she rested defenseless in her slumber. Sitting in the passenger's seat, a stocky built woman with red hair, Blanche's Aunt Rachel, sat contentedly in conversation with the handsome driver who usually ignored her boring testimony. It was only a quarter mile until the family reached the comfort of their home where a fire could be built to ward off the cold creeping through the cracks of the thin glass windows.

Blanche was startled by a jolt she received when the car ran over a pothole in the road. After adjusting her eyes, she looked straight ahead expecting to see the white framed house where she could once more close her eyes and return to a world where all cares are forgotten.

Instead of seeing the house where she lived, she saw a small creature appear from nowhere. It seemed to have jumped from the side of the road onto the hood of the car. Blanche watched in amazement as the figure poised itself in a hunched over position watching the family intently. There seemed to be a fire in his eyes reflecting off the chrome attached to the hood of the car.

A grin fell across the creature's face with his lips parting, producing jagged teeth hugging a black flickering tongue. Slowly the creature stretched out his bony arm and pointed a small finger in Aunt Rachel's direction.

Blanche stared at the hood of the car in a state of shock, not believing what she had just seen. As quickly as he had appeared, the monster vanished into thin air leaving everyone occupying the car with an ashen face. It was not only Blanche who had seen the devil but all of her relatives as well.

Two weeks later a call came with disturbing news that Aunt Rachel had fallen mysteriously ill and died. Everyone looked at each other remembering the creature on the hood of the car and the age-old legend of Louisville.

Rosemary Hall

ROSEMARY HALL

Visitors to North Augusta have entertained themselves since the early 1900s at Rosemary Hall. Today it plays host as a bed and breakfast, and the ambience of old southern charm remains unspoiled. Events are held at the building weekly with weddings being a favorite occasion.

Rosemary Hall dates to 1902 and was owned by the founder of North Augusta, South Carolina, James Urquardt Jackson. He contracted Woodward Lumber Company to build the house.

There is a beautiful illustration of Greek Revival architecture in the home with twelve massive Corinthian columns supporting a frieze of acanthus leaves. Porches stretch around the exterior of the home where a visitor can relax in a rocking chair and sip a glass of cool tea on a warm spring day.

Throughout the house, every turn provides glimpses of beautiful woodwork, especially the English stairway leading to the upper floors. Legend says the homeowner handpicked the rosemary pine used to build the staircase from thirty carloads of lumber.

James Jackson was an influential and wealthy man whose resume spans cotton brokerage, real estate, and hotel management. In 1916, his dreams of success in hotel management were burned along with a fire that destroyed the Wade Hampton Terrace. Even today the city of North Augusta remembers the grand hotel that once stood proud, attracting wealthy visitors from the north.

It was presumably a favorable action to know people with influence, and James Jackson was not a stranger to people of motivation. He knew major league baseball players, wealthy businessmen, and movie stars. During cold winter months snow would blanket the Detroit area and hold it in an icy grip, so to relieve themselves from winter's breath and take a well deserved vacation, the Detroit Tigers rented rooms at Rosemary Hall.

Using the connections that he had, James Jackson started working on a project to bring film making to North Augusta. The area was ideal for such a venture because of the warm climate and mild winters. Despite a small interest from people in the industry and his boldest attempts, the project did not bear fruit and failed.

Rosemary Hall stayed in the Jackson family for many years, at one time four Jackson families lived in the home. In 1983, the home was sold to Bill and Millie Thompson, who did renovation work to the home, helping to preserve its southern beauty. Later the home was sold to Japanese investors and was converted into a bed and breakfast. The new inn was again put up for sale and was soon purchased by the current owner, who also owns Lookaway Hall across the street, and runs both buildings as a bed and breakfast.

Over the years since the house was converted into a bed and breakfast, stories have evolved about James Jackson's wife being seen inside the inn. Visitors have reported seeing a short old woman on the main stairs leading up to the second floor. Some have reported seeing her on the second floor walking around. Guests and former employees usually tell of her appearing in a peaceful state, but at times she plays the prankster by moving objects from one place to another around the house.

North Augusta hosts many beautiful homes from the past, but none can compare to the beauty of Rosemary Hall except the sister house across the street. Each has an impressive flair. Mrs. Jackson often comes to check on the activities happening in and around the home that has meant so much to her family in the past. Quietly, she may peak in on guests to see how they are enjoying their stay, always leaving with a smile.

AUGUSTA'S PRESIDENT

Dust hovered in the air from horse-drawn wagons and carriages clogging the dry dirt road in front of the First Presbyterian Church on Telfair Street. A new pastor, Joseph Ruggles Wilson, had been sent to Augusta to lead the church and congregation. Along with the newcomer was his wife Janet, two daughters Annie and Marion, and son Thomas.

Thomas Woodrow Wilson, known affectionately as Tommy, was a year old when he arrived in Augusta with his family. A manse was provided to the Wilson family where they lived for a brief period. Two years later a new manse was constructed across street from the First Presbyterian Church.

Tommy spent his childhood growing up in Augusta. His father utilized the city as a giant classroom, full of knowledge waiting to be opened. Several days a week were spent exploring areas of Augusta. Tommy was taken to the Confederate Powder Works, the pistol factory, the Arsenal, and several cotton mills. Everyday events were taken into account as possible lessons to be learned.

Every day Tommy waited anxiously for his father to return home from his pastoral duties and read to him. His father's words took Tommy into a world of adventure. By age nine, it was time for Tommy to start his formal education. During this time he would learn his vocabulary, but it was not until eleven years of age that the ability to read would start to develop. Tommy had problems with his studies and had to work hard to compete with his peers. Modern day researchers found that he suffered from dyslexia. His father played an active roll in his education even into adulthood. Tommy later in life referred to his father as the greatest teacher he had ever had.

One of the gifts Tommy's father bestowed on him was the ability to speak publicly. After a visit to one of Augusta's educational stops, the elder Wilson would have his son speak out loud about his experience. Instilling in him the ability to speak in a clear and concise manner, along with giving detail in what he would say followed him through his life prompting many of his successes. He excelled in oratory and debate while concentrating on his formal education.

Georgia succeeded from the Union, and on April 12, 1861 the Civil War began against northern aggression. Tommy's father supported the war effort and the Southern cause. Certainly the young boy was kept up to date on all happenings that transpired throughout the years of the war by the teaching efforts of his father. Growing up through the Civil War and Reconstruction weighed heavily on Tommy. Even as an adult he was often silent about the topic and never spoke much about it.

Tommy witnessed many events such as his father's church being turned into a hospital for wounded soldiers. Union prisoners were also kept on the church grounds. When he was four years old, his first recollection was hearing of Abraham Lincoln's winning election to the Presidency of the United States, and rumors of war on the horizon.

General Robert E. Lee visited Augusta after the war was over. Tommy knew of his coming and was anxious to get a glimpse of the famous war hero. As the figure moved through the massive crowd engulfing the streets, Tommy knew he had to get closer, so squeezing and working his way through the crowd he finally made his way next to the general. What was said to Tommy by General Lee, if anything, is unknown.

Another event witnessed by Tommy was the arrival of fallen Confederate President Davis. When the president was brought through Augusta, he was shackled and surrounded by Union soldiers enroute to Savannah where he would begin a voyage up the East Coast to where he would become imprisoned for his acts during the war.

Tommy's relatives lived on "The Hill" outside of Augusta near the Arsenal. Union soldiers took control of the Arsenal after the war. Tommy and his friends would see the soldiers and in their young impressionable minds Yankees were evil men. So setting wheels in motion he began to think. Soon he came up with an idea. Everyone knew that Presbyterians were good, so all that had to be done was to convert the soldiers over to his religion, then all of them would become good and proper men. It is improbable that the soldiers were converted, but in a young child's eyes after witnessing the devastation of war, a dream is not such a bad thing.

In the hayloft of the carriage house behind the two-story structure that housed a loving family, the Lightfoot Baseball Club met, with Tommy as the president. Sitting beside him at every meeting were his devoted friends, especially his best childhood friend Joseph Lamar. Joseph and Tommy lived next door to each other while growing up, and would later in life share political success together.

At age fourteen Tommy and his family left the manse to move to Columbia, South Carolina, where his father took a job as a professor at a theology school. Later in life

Tommy would change his name to Woodrow Wilson, using only his middle and last names because he did not think he would be taken seriously with the nickname given to him as a child. Eventually he would become president of Princeton and Governor of New Jersey. He proved to be an accomplished author with the publication of several works of literature. His final feat was to win the popular vote and become the twenty-eighth President of the United States on November 5, 1913.

While campaigning for the presidency, Woodrow Wilson made one final stop in Augusta to relax for a weekend. He visited his old home, took a stroll down the streets he played in as a child, and saw a play that featured baseball great Ty Cobb. This was a time he could once again be just Tommy.

President Wilson wanted peace, but the attempt was only in vain. There was a four-year period in which he tried to keep the United States out of World War I. Because he witnessed the horrors of war, there is no doubt his experiences in Augusta shaped his views and prompted him to become a man that left his legacy in Augusta that has become legend. After the war President Wilson would receive the Nobel Peace Prize for his efforts to bring unity to the world.

Augusta influenced the character of a President. Woodrow Wilson never forgot the years he spent in Georgia. For a short time he practiced law in Atlanta, and received admission to the Georgia bar. Even his first wife, Ellen Louise Axson, was a Georgia resident, whom he met in Rome, Georgia. So throughout his life President Wilson always had a connection to the South.